Healing Katrina

Volunteering in Post-Hurricane Mississippi

Timothy H. Warneka

Asogomi Publishing International
Cleveland, Ohio

Cover & Interior Design by Asogomi Publishing International.

The purpose of this book is to educate and entertain. Although the author and publisher have made every effort to ensure the accuracy and completeness of information contained in this book, we assume no responsibility for errors, inaccuracies, omissions, or any inconsistency herein. Any slights of written material, people, places or organizations are unintentional. Names and other identifying information have sometimes been change to protect people.

The views contained in this book belong solely to the author. This book has in no way been endorsed or approved by the American Red Cross.

First printing 2007.
Cover Design by: Asogomi Publishing International
Editor: Cheri Laser
All pictures © Timothy H. Warneka

LCCN: 2006907478
ISBN: 978-0-9768627-3-4

Published by:
Asogomi Publishing International,
P.O. Box 20, Cleveland, Ohio 44092
(440) 944-4746

SPECIAL SALES:
Asogomi Publishing International books are available at special bulk purchase discounts to use for sales promotion, premiums, gifts, increasing magazine subscriptions or renewals, and educational purposes. Special books or book excerpts can also be created to fit specific needs. For information, please contact Asogomi Publishing International, P.O. Box 20, Cleveland, OH 44092, or email the us at: Sales@asogomi.com.

This book is dedicated to everyone impacted
by the 2005 Hurricane season—
especially the wonderful people
of the great state of Mississippi
and the volunteers who served them.

Certificate of Appreciation

This certificate recognizes

Timothy Warneka

for your valuable service during
the 2005 hurricane season relief efforts

Bonnie McElveen-Hunter
Chairman

Jack McGuire
President and CEO

American Red Cross
Together, we can save a life

C908
November 2005

Preface

Preface

In the autumn of 2005, I had the privilege of volunteering with the American Red Cross (ARC) in the devastating aftermath of Hurricanes Katrina and Rita, part of the worst hurricane season ever on record. I was deployed as a mental health professional along the southern coast of Mississippi—where Katrina had hit the hardest. During my volunteer stint, I kept both a hand-written journal as well as an electronic blog that formed the core of this book.

I wrote this book with the intention of helping raise awareness of the extensive damage caused by the storms of 2005. I want to encourage people to understand that—U.S. media coverage to the contrary—far more cities, towns and villages beyond New Orleans were impacted by the 2005 Hurricane Season. Before I left Ohio, many people I spoke to automatically assumed I was being sent to New Orleans when they heard that I had volunteered with the ARC. When I was volunteering in Mississippi, I spoke to many residents who were angered at the extensive (almost exclusive) media coverage of the damage in New Orleans, as if nowhere else had been impacted by the storms. Of course, this is in no way meant to minimize the tragedy that struck New Orleans, but instead is meant to broaden people's understanding that more than 90,000 square miles—an area roughly the size of Great Britain—was devastated by the storms of 2005.

This was a very difficult book for me to write. When I returned from the south, my intention was to type up my journal immediately. But I discovered the experience to be so emotionally provocative that I needed to wait more than 10 months for the feelings to settle. I have purposely left my journal and blog entries only roughly polished and edited in this book in order to give the reader a sense of what the circumstances were like: raw, repetitive and overwhelming.

I for one was certainly overwhelmed by my experience. In an attempt to come to terms with what I encountered, as I wrote this book I found myself researching statistics on the impact of the 2005 Hurricane season. Statistics without context being meaningless, I have chosen another national event as a comparison for the numbers that I found—the on-going war in Iraq. The numbers might surprise you.

During my time as a volunteer, there were days when Internet access was not available. Fortunately, by the time I arrived in the south— about five weeks after the storm—most of the cell phone infrastructure had been repaired, so I was usually able to call out. Consequently, there were times when I would call my brother (Patrick) or sister (Mary), who would then post to the blog. I have noted in the book when either of them authored a particular blog.

Even now, almost a year later, there is still so much work to be done. The government reports that 97% of the debris from the storm has been removed (where did they put it all?). Now the rebuilding can take place in earnest. Rebuilding the physical scars will take years. Healing the emotional and psychological scars will take longer.

I hope that you find something valuable in these pages.

T.H.W.
Cleveland, OH.

Leaving

Friday, September 23, 2005
Blog

Leaving on a Jet Plane

Morning! I'm outward bound for Montgomery, Alabama. A friend was going to drop me off at the airport, but luckily, the school where my wife works didn't have power/phones, so my wife and kids will be able to take me to the airport instead.

The last week has been very stressful. Very busy. Imagine what you would have to do to go away for two weeks with only about a seven-day notice. So many details! I'm looking forward to the flight just to be able to sit still for a few moments.

This journey is my first time as a volunteer with the American Red Cross (ARC), so I'm feeling anxious and a bit overwhelmed. I hope I can help the people where I am going. My intention is also to treat this as a two-week meditation retreat. Stillness in action.

I hope to be able to blog more from wherever I end up being assigned. If there is web access, I'll blog. Otherwise, my brother Patrick and sister Mary will be blogging for me.

I ask everyone to please keep me and everyone else down South in your prayers, thoughts and meditations.

Katrina
At a Glance

The name *Katrina* was retired in the spring of 2006 by the World Meterological Organization and will never be used again to name a hurricane in the Atlantic basin.

Friday, September 23, 2005 Blog

At Least, I *Thought* I Was Leaving…

This morning my wife and kids dropped me off at the Cleveland airport, which was very busy due to weather conditions caused by the approach of Hurricane Rita. A number of flights had been stranded overnight in Cleveland. Every counter had people trying to find flights out so they could get home. I waited in line to check in, only to find that my flight had been cancelled. With all of this going on, the airlines had only two clerks working! They took 45 minutes to get through eight people! Wow.

Luckily, a friend loaned me her cell phone (thanks Kirste!), so I was able to call my wife and have her come back to pick me up.

After several calls to the American Red Cross travel agency, I was able to get through and found that the next logical flight out was Monday. Saturday flights are all jammed up, as they expect the storm to hit sometime on Saturday. Modern air travel is truly a systemic adventure—problems anywhere in the country cause a ripple effect that impacts everywhere else in the country (and probably the world, to some extent).

Basically, the long and short of it is that I was just granted an unexpected weekend with my family! Also, I had intentionally delayed sending my book, *Leading People the Black Belt Way*, to print because I was not able to prepare for the trip south and to also adequately prepare the book for printing. Now, I'm excited to say, I should be able to complete the work on the book this weekend, and it'll be prepared for printing while I am gone.

These past few days have been very emotionally exhausting for me. I plan on going home, taking a nap and having fun with my kids this weekend—and cutting the grass, most likely.

My heart goes out to all the travel agents and airline personnel who are working hard to get people home as well as getting Red Cross people where they need to be. I'm sure everyone's thoughts and prayers are with the people in Hurricane Rita's path.

Sunday, September 25, 2005
Blog

Trying Again ...

It's Sunday night, and hopefully I will be flying out tomorrow, sometime early in the afternoon. I had an enjoyable weekend—got to watch a movie with my kids, practice Aikido (a martial art), and play Super Scrabble with my wife and some good friends. Oh, and I cut the grass, too. I was also able to take care of a number of other small details, including the final steps toward getting my book published. Overall, I feel *much* less harried about leaving.

The American Red Cross (ARC) has been having daily conference/bridgeline calls for people to call in and get information about deployment. I listened in on the calls on both Friday and Saturday. There was a great deal of re-deployment and cancellations of trips (would that be considered *un-deployment?* This ARC terminology is still new to me) due to hurricane Rita. I don't envy the ARC officials this weekend—I'm sure they are facing some enormous logistical nightmares.

For those of you keeping track, my return date is still the same—Friday, Oct. 7th, 2005.

Katrina
At a Glance

In the 2005 Hurricane season, the American Red Cross opened up 1,196 shelters.

Monday, September 26, 2005
Journal

Morning, In the Air Over Ohio

There's an old Chinese saying that goes something like, "The only difference between a brave person and a cowardly person is the direction they are running." As I write this, I am in the air flying somewhere over Ohio, southbound for Memphis, Tennessee and on from there to Montgomery, Alabama. Using my skills as a mental health professional, executive coach and organizational consultant, I hope to alleviate some of the emotional trauma that is occurring there. (I'm praying that my skills as a martial artist will lie dormant.)

I am feeling pretty overwhelmed and frightened at this point in time. This will be the longest that I've ever been away from my wife and kids (my son just turned 10, so that feels like a long time). I volunteered through the National ARC, so I'm headed off by myself. A number of people from the local ARC chapter went off together in teams, but I'm solo. Before I left, I spoke to a friend who is a nurse at the Cleveland Clinic. The Clinic will be sending down a response team and is now in the process of putting that team together. How different it would be to be going down as part of a team instead of as an individual. It's amazing how, when under stress, people look for familiar faces (present company included). But, the folks down South need my skills now, so I will travel alone.

My main intention in keeping this journal is to offer the world a glimpse of what it is like to respond to a national disaster with the ARC. At this point in time, I'd like to know that myself, as this is my first ARC deployment. I've responded to a few local crises, including a school shooting that made the national media several years ago, but certainly nothing on this scale. So, I make no claims that what is contained within this journal is at all a comprehensive understanding of a disaster response—it's only my experience.

I had intended to start this journal a week before I left, but I simply ran out of time. With young kids and my own business, I'm used to busy schedules. However, the week before I left (my *pre-deployment week* in ARC jargon) was fantastically hectic. I work independently as an executive coach, consultant and holistic counselor. I also teach a course and work part-time as an academic counselor at a local community college. Consequently, when I was preparing to leave, I had to negotiate my absence with several organizations, each responding in their own ways. Some of the organizations bent over backwards to support my going, while others responded in ways that seemed less helpful. Negotiating with each took time. I became very frustrated with the entire pre-deployment process, but each time I got frustrated, somewhere in the back of my head echoed the words of Dame Julian of Norwich: "All shall be well and all shall be well and all manner of things shall be well." Those words certainly got me through some rough spots.

So why *am* I going? I'm not entirely certain myself. Mostly because I can help, I suppose. "It's people helping people," a friend of mine told me, in what I imagine was a wise attempt to simplify my tendency to over-complicate things. I am going because I have the skills to help. I am going because my second grade daughter will be making her first communion this year, and we have been having discussions about what it means to "serve others." I want to walk my talk. I'm going because I was frustrated by the slow response of the relief efforts immediately after the storm. Most likely, I'm going for reasons that I won't begin to understand until later down the road.

In my communications with ARC, they have repeatedly referred to the *hardship conditions* that I will be going into—poor and highly stressful conditions. A lot of that is okay with me. For whatever reasons, I'm usually not overly concerned with creature comforts. For the most part, it doesn't really matter to me what I eat; it doesn't matter where I sleep. Of course, like everyone else, I have my eating and sleeping preferences, but when those conditions change, it doesn't seem to faze me as much as I see it affect some other people. So, poor physical conditions don't bother me. (As long as they are safe, of course.)

Having said all that, I'll admit that this entire journey is a psychological stretch for me. While adverse physical conditions don't tend to bother me, I personally do not deal well with the anxiety of ambiguous situations. So I'm amazed that I am even here—flying through the air, going to the largest natural disaster the U.S. has ever had—a situation that is ripe for ambiguity.

At another level, I think I'm headed south with the ARC in a continuing effort to cope with the impact of 9/11. After the terrorist attacks on the Twin Towers, I, along with so many other people, desperately wanted to do something—anything—to help. I felt a strong desire to get in my car and drive to New York City. But with a job and a wife and two young kids at home, I wasn't able to physically do anything, so I started writing. I wrote a short article entitled *Ten Tips for Talking About Terrorism with Your Kids* that was circulated around the web and published in several journals. That small writing project led to others, all the way up to my first book—*Leading People the Black Belt Way*. The irony is not lost on me that the launch of my book, which has its roots in 9/11, is being delayed because I am responding to another national disaster.

I want to use this journal to honestly present both the positive and negative parts of myself, lest I come across as too idealistic or noble. There were several days in my pre-deployment week when I felt absolutely terrified and certain that I should cancel the entire trip. As I mentioned, I am the type of person who experiences a high degree of anxiety around ambiguity. I usually don't do things unless there's a safety net, as well as a safety net under *that* safety net. My pre-deployment week was filled with uncertainty and anxiety. In fact, I wasn't even positive that I was even leaving until about two days before I left.

Also, when I'm honest, I even recognize a wee bit of narcissism in this whole process—in that it is "I" going to help the hurricane survivors/victims/relief workers. Through this process, I hope to focus more on the "we" of the project and less on the "I" of it all. (There's no "i" in "Red Cross," hey?)

My intention is also to use this time as a meditation retreat. I haven't been on a retreat in years—I simply cannot justify being away from my wife and kids for very long. I've heard of—and been impressed by—people who do five-day or ten-day retreats every year, religiously, even when their kids are young. While I think "Good for them," I'm clear that doing something similar is not for me. I used to feel guilty about not wanting to go on a yearly retreat, thinking that I was somehow short-changing my spirituality. Then it finally dawned on me—that parenting can be a form of meditative practice. Not always pleasant, or enjoyable (or quiet!), but it is a meditation practice nonetheless. Now that I am facing two weeks with the ARC, I'm challenging myself to practice meditation in action. Sort of like an intensive Aikido training (a non-violent martial art that I practice) except without the uniform, without the mats and without (most likely) a lot of other Aikido practitioners, which should turn up the heat a bit on me.

Most of all, I promise myself I'll breathe.

Monday, September 26, 2005 Journal

... A Little Later that Same Day ...

Still flying, I'm looking out the window at the gorgeous clouds beneath us. It's like riding through cotton balls or—for you Northerners—it's like looking out over a frozen lake in winter, with drifts of white snow and patches of blue where the frozen water (or sky, in this case) peek through.

Modern day flying always strikes me as quite odd. For thousands and thousands of years, people have looked to the skies and dreamt of flying. They wrote songs and myths and poems about flying. To the ancients, flying was filled with songs of the soul. We moderns invented flying—and immediately suck the soul out of it. Countless of our ancestors would have given a literal right arm to do what some of us do on a daily basis—leave the ground and lift high into the air. But we in our modern wisdom have turned flying into a cramped, crowded, tedious chore. Personally, I think we missed something somewhere.

I'm arriving in Memphis. Back soon.

Katrina
At a Glance

As of summer 2006, FEMA has provided assistance totaling $5,925,599,488 ($5.9 billion) over the past 41 weeks.

The Department of Defense is spending $6 to $9 billion every month on the war in Iraq.

Monday, September 26, 2005
Journal

Evening in Montgomery

The wait in the Memphis airport was fairly short, and then I flew to Montgomery, Alabama in a small jet. Met two other Red Cross volunteers getting on the same flight—one from South Dakota and the other from Minnesota. Montgomery is a small but pretty airport and flying in was beautiful. I've never been in Alabama before. After we got off the plane, we waited by the terminal for the Red Cross shuttle that would take us to the local headquarters. While we were waiting, I chatted with a police officer. It felt pretty hot to me, but he assured me that it was "cooling down for fall." He said that Montgomery had escaped the brunt of the storm, but there was still a lot of work to be done.

After getting picked up by an ARC volunteer, we drove to the Red Cross Headquarters (or *HQ* in ARC-speak). The shuttle driver, a friendly ARC volunteer from Idaho, assured us this would be a "life-changing" event (and he has been here only one week!). The HQ was set up in an old K-mart store. Checking in (or *in-processing* in ARC language) went pretty swiftly, but my attempted jokes about "blue light specials" were met with some blank stares by the workers. People seemed all business in the HQ, until I got to the Mental Health table, where I was immediately teased by Pat, a wonderful counselor from Virginia. Pat's job was checking in mental health workers, and I welcomed her teasing with a sigh of relief.

I settled down and even managed to grab a meal. Different church groups were coming in and serving the meals to the ARC folks. After the meal, I felt a little sad and lost. Sometimes, the more I slow down, the more I become aware of my feelings, instead of the usual rush of activity that I do to cover these feelings up. Here in the Montgomery, Alabama ARC HQ, there was nothing for me to do, so I sat with my feelings. Breathe.

Tomorrow I am scheduled for orientation, and then I may be deployed immediately. Or I may wait. Apparently one never knows with the ARC. I brought Ken Wilber's book *Sex, Ecology & Spirituality* with me to read while I'm waiting. It's a pretty thick book, but I find that non-fiction often settles me down more than reading fiction. (Consider it my intellectual security blanket.) Plus, I figured that carrying a thick book through a bureaucracy like the ARC would be like carrying an umbrella in northeastern Ohio. Whenever I carry an umbrella back home, it never seems to rain. It only seems to rain when my umbrella is in the car. I figured that if I carried a big thick book with me, I would probably never have to wait in a long line (which proved to be surprisingly true throughout the trip).

Tonight the ARC set me up in a hotel room, which I'm sharing with a psychologist from New York. Before I left the HQ, the staff told me, "Enjoy the air conditioning in your hotel room—it may be your last night with it." I always wondered what Southern nights felt like and it looks like I'm about to find out. I did take a short walk outside so that I could call my family and some friends on a cell phone that my dear friend Kirste lent me. It was wonderful hearing my kids' voices. Although far from a Luddite, I've managed to avoid carrying a cell phone so far—they feel so intrusive. Now that I'm here, I think cell phones are pretty amazing. Most of all, I miss my kids.

Tuesday, September 27, 2005
Blog

Tuesday Morning

Morning! I'm blogging as I wait at the hotel for the ARC shuttle back to HQ. Today is orientation day so I'm sure I'll be learning lots. Slept well last night—an air conditioned hotel room was more than I was expecting! Hope this wasn't my last shower for the week.

More to follow.

Katrina
At a Glance

In the 2005 Hurricane season,
the American Red Cross provided
801,280 mental health services
contacts.

Tuesday, September 27, 2005
Journal

7:20 a.m.

I am back at the old K-mart, otherwise known as ARC HQ, sitting off to one side in a folding chair. The place is slowly starting to come alive. I got up early to catch a shuttle here (as I was told that the shuttles ran sporadically, so it was best to catch an early one). Orientation doesn't start for another hour. I can feel a bit of panic rising—it's really weird to be in a situation where I barely know what is going to happen two hours from now, let alone tomorrow.

It's very funny how, at home, I often chafe against the braces of a "dull" routine—taking care of the kids, working, taking care of the house, and all the rest. Now that I am off on somewhat of an adventure, I long for a normal day at home. I think it was the Western writer, Louis L'Amour, who said something like, "Adventure is just a romantic name for trouble." Smart guy, that Louie.

As I write, I can feel the panic subsiding. Breathe. The panic—the anxiety—again seems to be about not being able to *do* something. At home, if I have a task that I am familiar with, then I can do it under almost any conditions. But put me in a place where there is little to do—*that* I find much more difficult. Right now, I find myself really wishing that I'd come down as part of a team. A familiar face would be quite welcome.

This loneliness reminds me of high school—like being the new kid in school all over again. There are people here at HQ who are quite familiar with each other, and then there are a lot of new kids—people coming in from the airport and other places. The obvious logical move for me is to connect with other new kids, but I'm feeling more introspective and quiet (and probably overwhelmed), and so I'll continue to write. I don't seem to have the energy to introduce myself to more people.

I was speaking to another ARC volunteer this morning who was here over the weekend, and he said they evacuated this ARC HQ because of tornado warnings that were connected with Rita. It sounded like it was fairly chaotic this past weekend, so I'm glad that my flight was delayed back home. I was lucky—I got to spend another two days with my family, which, although wonderful, was also strange in that I can't remember that last time I had two completely unscheduled days. All weekend long I kept thinking that I needed to be somewhere, doing something. I spoke to some other ARC workers who got stranded in various airports when Rita hit, so I felt very lucky to have been near home.

Tuesday, September 27, 2005
Blog

Waiting for Deployment

Hi all! Tuesday afternoon. I made it through several orientation sessions. The Red Cross really has this well organized (especially given the conditions). Overall, the presenters have been really good, especially the mental health presenter.

Some facts that I learned today:

• Katrina is the largest disaster in the 125-year history of the Red Cross.

• The Red Cross has served more than 12 million hot meals in the Katrina response so far.

• To date, more than 328,000 people have received Red Cross disaster mental health services

• To date, more than 147,000 trained Red Cross disaster relief workers from all 50 states, Puerto Rico and the Virgin Islands have responded to Katrina.

Wow. These numbers are simply staggering to me. It's really overwhelming (in a good sense, though) being in a large group of people, all of whom have the intention of helping out. Amazing.

I am doing well. It's hot down here, and there's a lot of hustle-bustle as people prepare to deploy. I'm on a roller coaster ride of emotions, from excited to overwhelmed and everywhere in between. Things are moving really quickly, so I want to apologize if I repeat anything on these blogs.

I just found out that I'm being deployed tomorrow, so I gotta go get my assignment.

See ya!

Tuesday, September 27, 2005
Journal

... Meanwhile, Back at the Ranch ...

A very busy day. Orientation kept me hopping. During the general orientation, the ARC facilitator (a wonderfully warm woman from Minnesota) was very clear that this was a hardship situation and that we could leave now if we weren't aware of that. The ARC facilitators seem to stress *hardship* over and over. All of the orientation presenters were top notch, which is something of a rarity these days. My hat goes off to the ARC for how they've organized the presenters. I spoke to one supervisor who told me that the ARC was processing between 300-400 people per day through Montgomery. That's a lot of Red Cross volunteers. I saw that they also brought in a large number of temporary workers to process the data entry end of things.

I've met some very wonderful people here: a woman from Michigan whose gentle teasing keeps me from taking things too seriously; a mental health trainer with a strong ability to provide an enormous amount of valuable information over a short time; and a man from Washington State who's eyes sparkle when he tells a joke. There's a whole age range of people here, from college students to senior citizens.

Most of the mental health workers who I came in with were deployed today. They must have something different in mind for me. Rumor has it that ARC is starting a place with 30–50 mental health professionals somewhere near Hattiesburg, Mississippi. I spent the afternoon organizing my gear and doing minor bureaucratic tasks. Then I was told that I was being deployed to Biloxi. When I told my Hattiesburg-bound colleagues where I was going, they teased me about being quite jealous of not getting to go with me. Ignorant of geography as I am, I sought out a map and located Biloxi. I discovered that I am going to be right on the Gulf, very close to where Katrina made landfall. In other words—Ground Zero.

I am being deployed to Biloxi with two other ARC volunteers—John from Illinois and Teresa from Alaska. We are all staying at the same hotel tonight, so we went out to dinner together. It was a great evening, part of which we spent telling our stories about how each of us got here. What really struck me was how similar our stories were—especially the alternating doubt, excitement and chaos in the week(s) before deployment. Now it's time to go off to bed. Got a big day ahead of me as we drive from Montgomery, Alabama to Biloxi, Mississippi.

Wednesday, September 28, 2005
Journal

Morning Reflections

Good morning. I'm reflecting on how the Red Cross uses language. I am fascinated by language—the tool of coaches, therapists and teachers. The Red Cross, like most other organizations, has its own unique language. A sociologist would have a field-day in this place. What strikes me most about the ARC language is how military it is. One sign near me even reads, "An army of healing." In the Red Cross, home base is called *headquarters* or simply *HQ*; volunteers are *deployed*, often in *teams* or *units*. Meetings are *briefings*, and there is talk of *battlefield promotions*. Volunteers *in-process* when they arrive and *out-process* when they leave.

There is a whole wealth of other acronyms and abbreviations here, most of which I'm still trying to figure out. The event itself—Hurricane Katrina in this case—is referred to as a *D.R.*, which is short for *D.R.O.*, which stands for *Disaster Relief Operations*. A D.R. typically receives one number. Hurricane Katrina is so large that it received several D.R.O. numbers. I am in D.R. #871 (which, in ARC-speak, each number is said individually: "eight-seven-one", never "eight-seventy-one"). My understanding is that my team (myself, Teresa and John) are being "loaned" to a different D.R. when we go to Biloxi, which, for some reason quite beyond my ken, appears to be a very big deal around HQ right now. Several individuals up the ARC food chain have come to me and told me how important it is that this team is being "loaned out." In these discussions, I nod my head and try to look serious, although I don't grasp all the nuances about why this fact is important.

Continuing with the language theme, I've noticed that D.R.O.'s are also commonly referred to by a name, so this event is referred to either as "871" or "Katrina." When ARC volunteers meet for the first time, a common question is some variation of, "Which other D.R.'s have you been deployed on?" First-timers like me (of which there are many down here) reply, "None." The more experienced volunteers can begin quite a list—many events with which I have no familiarity or that I vaguely remember hearing something about on the news at the time.

Most ARC volunteers tend to talk about disasters where they've been deployed in a very matter-of-fact way. Except for 9/11. When I speak to ARC volunteers who deployed in 9/11, then we are in a different ball game. When they talk about "9/11," the ARC volunteers who were there all seem to tense up and often look away. Their eyes, when I can catch them, seem to hold a great deal of pain—the suffering of a nation. Just by conversing with the experienced ARC volunteers, it is clear that the 9/11 D.R.O. seemed to impact people in a much deeper way than other events.

Off to deployment now.

Wednesday, September 28, 2005
Blog

Awaiting Departure to Biloxi

Morning all! It's 8:45 a.m. and I'm at the ARC HQ awaiting deployment to Biloxi. (That last sentence sounded rather military, no?!?). I'm going down with a good team, and I'll be right on the Mississippi coast, so it should be interesting. I was watching CNN last night, and they were doing some Red Cross bashing. From the inside, I want to say that I am absolutely amazed at what the ARC is doing. For a group of primarily volunteers working off donations, I think that they are incredibly organized given the conditions.

Be well.

Katrina
At a Glance

More than 1.5 million people were directly impacted by Hurricane Katrina.

Wednesday, September 28, 2005
Blog (by Patrick)

9:30 p.m. Central Time

Tim called just now—he sounds different. He is safe and well-fed at a military base in Gulfport, Mississippi. Tim said it is lights out at 10 p.m. and lights on at 6 a.m. on the base. He is sleeping in a warehouse on the base with about 700 people. Tim is teamed up with two other people, one woman and one man. They said they will stick together and watch out for each other—good! He said the drive was smooth but as they came close to Gulfport, he started to see rooftops missing and trees flattened.

When I spoke to him, Tim seemed to be a little pensive. He joked a bit on the phone but it sounded like he knew he was heading toward the epicenter of a big disaster. Tim is smart, fit and knows how to take care of himself, and I know we will give him some support when he gets back.

Go, Tim, go!

Katrina
At a Glance

By February, 2006,
the U.S. government had allocated
approximately $88 billion for relief,
recovery and rebuilding along
the Gulf Coast.

By February, 2006,
the U.S. government had allocated
approximately $225 billion
for the war in Iraq.

Wednesday, September 28, 2005
Journal

11:30 p.m., Gulfport

S hort entry, as this is written by flashlight. Drove down to
Biloxi, Mississippi with John and Teresa—a beautiful day
and a good trip. Saw increasing devastation as we got closer
to Biloxi. ARC HQ in Biloxi is in a Shriners' building. It took us
awhile to find HQ as most of the street signs have been blown
down. Sleeping quarters are 600–700 people on cots in a Seabees
warehouse on a military base in Gulfport.

As we had been driving for most of the day, the three of
us got quite slap-happy on the drive over to the base—laughing hysterically at some very childish jokes. At the base, we were
welcomed by a wonderfully warm man from New York. Had a
flashlight meeting with supervisor who prepped us so that we
could hit the ground running the next day. "Battlefield promotions" happen quickly here, but I wonder—do I want to be a
leader in this situation?

Time will tell. Good night.

Katrina
At a Glance

More than 233,768 people volunteered with the American Red Cross in the 2005 hurricane season.

Considering an average 3-week volunteer rotation, that comes to over 13,486 years of donated time!

Thursday, September 29, 2005
Journal

5:25 a.m.

Slept on a cot in a Seabee warehouse with 700+ of my closest friends. We are all on cots spaced about two feet apart. Restrooms are port-a-toilets, and the showers are enormous portable shower trailers. Got up at 4:30 a.m ... by choice. We're in Central Standard Time and my biological clock is still on Eastern Standard Time, so it was 5:30 a.m. for me. At home, I usually get up between 5:30–6:00 a.m., so that was about right. If I understood my supervisor's briefing yesterday, today I will be working at a place that is handing out checks to families.

This encampment—for lack of a better term—is amazing: 600–700 people living in very close quarters (for Americans), all volunteers, and all seem to be doing fairly well.

I find my thoughts to be jumping around this morning. I didn't get to talk to my kids yesterday, so I'm hoping to get in a quick call this morning. I feel sad and I miss them. The work down here is important, too, so off I go.

I have spoken to several people here and already have heard horror stories about previous mental health workers. It seems that some mental health workers, while well-meaning, had been a bit overzealous, shall we say, running around with clip boards and asking people if they were "mentally O.K." Exactly the wrong way to approach staff. Aikido, the non-violent martial art I train in, teaches finding less directive—yet more effective—ways of dealing with people. I think a more Aikido-oriented approach would work better here. Also hearing reports of theft in the staff shelters. Gotta watch my stuff.

Last night in briefing, my supervisor mentioned that she would try and get someone to take us down to the coast so we could see the devastation firsthand. When another new worker pointed out that he had seen a lot of devastation on his trip down, and didn't feel like taking a "field trip", the supervisor made the excellent point that her intention was *not* to have us sightseeing. She firmly believed that it is important for us—as mental health workers—to have a firsthand experience of what has gone on here, so that we can more fully appreciate what these folks are facing. All of which will help us help people even better. I agree with that perspective very much.

Thursday, September 29, 2005
Blog

Driving Around Gulfport

Hi all! I had to talk quickly to Patrick last night—didn't have much power on my cell phone. I am spending evenings and nights at a Seabees Naval station near Gulfport. The cots in the warehouse are spaced about two feet apart. I managed to find a cot with my back to a wall, which helps my introverted self not to feel so freaked out by so many people!

I drove down from Montgomery with John from Illinois and Teresa from Alaska. We had some sun and drove through some rain. The closer we got to Biloxi, the more damage we could see. We spent the night in the shelter and got briefed by the mental health supervisor by flashlight at a 10:30 p.m. meeting (since it's lights out on the base at 10:00 p.m.).

We are using porta-toilets and showers on the back of a huge truck. This is an amazing setup, and even more unbelievable when I think that every person in that room is a volunteer! There are people of all ages, from college students to senior citizens. Everyone seems very friendly and supportive—I am quite certain that I was walking around in shock last night. It was a very surreal experience.

Today I am at the Biloxi HQ, which is operating out of a Shriners' building. They divide the coverage area out into "sectors," and I will be in a sector directly south of the Gulfport airport, right along the beach. I cannot even imagine what I am going to see.

I miss my family greatly, and send my kids and wife a big hug. I was able to call home before the kids left for school this morning, so that was nice. (My son scored a goal in soccer last night! Hooray!) This continues to be an amazing operation. Please keep us all in your prayers, and continue to financially support the American Red Cross and other similar organizations.

See ya!

Thursday, September 29, 2005
Blog (by Patrick)

Gulfport Blog

Tim called me tonight. Today he drove from Gulfport into part of Biloxi (but not the worst part). He said there was a great amount of destruction, and he has some pictures to show when he returns. He saw what was left of the guitar sign from the Hard Rock Cafe—the rest was destroyed. He also saw one of those casino boats that was washed ashore! The locals said that they had swells 28–30 feet high—yikes!

Tim says he is O.K. but is hot and has met some great people who need our help. Don't forget to check out the Red Cross website.

Katrina
At a Glance

Storm Surges in Mississippi

Bay St. Louis/Waveland: 34 feet
(10.4 m)
Gulfport: 24 feet (7.3 m)
Biloxi: 19 feet (5.8 m)
Pascagoula: 16 feet (4.9 m)

Reference Point

A single-story ranch house
averages 16-18 feet in height.

Saturday, October 1, 2005
Journal

Time Flies...

Whew! The days are flying by. I'm currently on mental health duty for the base (for the volunteers, at least). I was worried that this would be more light duty, but it has been pretty fast-paced all morning. The ARC mental health team here in Biloxi is very understaffed—there are about fifty-some of us to cover a three-county area. We could triple our staff and still be busy. Everyone is doing the best they can, but it can get frustrating at times.

There is *so* much to write about. On Thursday, I drove around Biloxi doing a form of case-management-on-steroids known as *community outreach* in ARC parlance. I was teamed up with a marvelous lady named Page from New York who showed me the ropes. We worked very hard that day—driving around the neighborhoods, passing out cold drinks and talking to people. We spent a good portion of the day getting medications for a mentally ill man living in the community. For those of you who have never done case management, "getting medications" may sound like a simple task, but under emergency conditions it can be incredibly time-consuming.

Before Page and I returned to HQ, we drove along Route 90, which runs right along the coast. The devastation was amazing. Words simply fail. Stately old antebellum houses just gone. Huge floating casinos pushed onto shore. Simply tragic.

When I was in Montgomery, I was watching an interview with the senators from Mississippi. They were requesting an enormous amount of money in aid. (I can't remember the exact figure.) At the time, the amount they were asking for seemed so large that I remember thinking, "What can you possibly do with that much money?" After driving along Route 90 today, however, I am quite certain that those senators did not ask for enough.

After working all day on Thursday, I went back to HQ where I was going to meet John and Teresa. Our lines got crossed and I ended up missing them, so I grabbed a ride back to base with a wonderful gentleman from Pennsylvania who proudly told me about his new granddaughter as we drove.

On Friday, I had the enormous pleasure of being teamed up with Bob, a very wise man who has been down here one month—two weeks longer than he planned. An ex-Marine and an experienced ARC volunteer, Bob had served as chaplain in the 9/11 morgue. Bob took me to East Biloxi, a portion of the town that had been completely devastated. Most of East Biloxi is in shambles, and entire neighborhoods are simply missing. Bob showed me a part of town that he referred to as "Hiroshima." Bob was right—it looked exactly like pictures I have seen of Hiroshima and Nagasaki, with blocks of houses simply blown away. The emotional impact of such a sight was simply overwhelming. I stopped taking pictures. I felt torn between wanting to run away screaming and wanting to move down here and stay for six months to help re-build.

Even now, five weeks after the storm, East Biloxi is still undersupplied and understaffed. As I'm supposed to take Bob's place as ARC worker in East Biloxi, Bob introduced me to a number of people—residents and volunteers alike, and I began to get a sense of what was needed. *A lot.* Like Bob, I found the lack of supplies and personnel to be very frustrating.

Even in the midst of devastation, I met amazing people—a contractor and his wife standing outside of their demolished home, joking with me about eating raw oysters and cold beer; a local Red Cross volunteer playfully teasing me about being a *cup-cake*—someone new to the area who has the look of devastation in their eyes; meeting a young boy the same age as my son (one of the first children I've seen all week) and thinking that, under different circumstances, how my son and this boy could be best of friends. Bob and I returned to HQ so that Bob could outprocess. We had lunch and I said goodbye as he left for the airport. At HQ, I began to do what years of community mental health work had trained me to do: to advocate for the underserved—this time for supplies for East Biloxi.

As I began to advocate, I was assigned some minor but time-consuming tasks by the staff at HQ. In the course of completing a task, I met a nurse in medical services who had just been to East Biloxi and was as frustrated about the lack of supplies and services there as I was. Together, we brainstormed several possible strategies and began advocating for East Biloxi as a team. Shortly thereafter—due to a staff illness—I was assigned to a *Family Services Center* (FSC), one of the places where they were distributing checks to local residents. I signed out an ARC van and drove to the FSC. When I arrived, I discovered that the FSC had run out of drinks for the people (who were waiting in the hot sun), so I unloaded all 10 cases of drinks that I had in the van. I stayed at the FSC until about 6:30 p.m. The FSC was being run by a young man who was clearly out of his league (but sadly, couldn't recognize it), and there was some conflict about how long the mental health workers had to stay on site. I, for one, had been working non-stop since early morning and was ready for dinner. As things were quiet, we mental health workers discussed the matter. After several calls to our supervisors (who we were not able to reach), my colleagues and I decided to return to the base for dinner. We left our cell phone numbers with the FSC supervisor and returned to base.

By the time I got back to base, I was so exhausted that I didn't trust myself to park the van in the tight quarters (I'm not the best driver even under normal conditions!). Luckily, one of the National Forest Service folks who was performing crowd control on base (which included directing traffic), was more than willing to park the van for me. I will never forget his kindness on that evening.

I went in and grabbed some dinner. Earlier in the week, Teresa, John and I had agreed to always touch base with each other in the evening in order to support our own mental health. I was very glad to process the day's events with Teresa, who was kind enough to listen. John left a message saying that he was involved in an emergency psychiatric hospitalization and that he would be late. I waited up until 11:30 p.m. when he returned to the base. We talked awhile to debrief, then I meditated and went to sleep.

Returning to the present day, today I was assigned to the base, working the mental health site for staff. While there is a corner of the room set aside for mental health concerns, my approach—following the time-honored social work perspective—is to go out and meet the people where they are. Some mental health workers chose to sit in the mental health area and wait for people to come to them. I'm not criticizing that approach, but I do think that it somewhat misses the boat. The morning was pretty busy—I had several crisis calls that I had to manage. Nothing too interesting, but important work nonetheless. The afternoon slowed down, so I took a nap and then created some posters for the mental health area, with outreach and humor being the focus.

When John and Teresa returned, we went to visit the dolphins who are being housed on base (from a local aquarium that had been destroyed in the storm), and then went to dinner. After dinner I went for a walk around the base. The day had been hot and sunny, but the evening was much cooler with a breeze blowing. Beautiful. I came back and worked the staff shelter some more—greeting and welcoming people and trying to support the shelter staff as much as I could. There really is an amazing bunch of people here. I spoke to one of the shelter staff who said that there were between 700–800 total volunteers currently on base and that they were looking at having 1,700 volunteers by next week. When I introduce myself, people say that there are a lot of folks from Ohio here, but I'm mainly meeting people from California, New York, Oregon and Washington State. I guess it depends on who you run into. Now off to bed.

Katrina
At a Glance

In the 2005 Hurricane season, the U.S. Coast Guard rescued 33,000 people—an amount six times higher than the total number of rescues the Coast Guard performed in 2004.

Saturday, October 1, 2005
Blog (by Mary)

October 1

Tim called around 9:15 this morning. His cell reception was good. After just four days, it seems like he has experienced enough already for a lifetime. His take on the American Red Cross is that they are amazing, organized and doing *so* much to bring relief to the area and yet, at the same time, they can be floundering, disorganized and have *so* many more things that they could be doing.

Tim mentioned some other groups that are working alongside the ARC down there—the Scientologists, and a group of Smoke Jumpers (firefighters from the National Forest Service who parachute in to combat fires and carry supplies) and other groups. As it turns out, the Smoke Jumpers bring their own caterers and portable shower facilities when they travel. Tim and the other volunteers have been enjoying well-cooked meals of BBQ ribs, shrimp, and Cajun dinners as well as being able to use the shower unit, which he described as a giant mobile home constructed as a shower house.

Part of Tim's support network—consisting of John from Illinois and Teresa from Alaska—continue to be stationed in the same area (even if they go their separate ways in the field during the day). They seem to be able to provide much needed processing time to one another. Tim also mentioned a fantastic ally he met, a chaplain from the Washington, DC area who had been working by himself to support a rather large area. Tim remarked that his friend's sense of humor and perseverance was a bright spot for him, even though the good chaplain has since returned home after a four-week stint.

Tim seemed steady and determined, as the rock that he is. He is seemingly able to hold his own sense of being overwhelmed at bay so he can be there for others. He does not have Internet access currently, but we'll continue to keep everybody posted through Patrick's ingenuity. He's got seven days and, I'm sure, a lifetime of experiences left.

Sending best wishes of courage and positive energy.

Sunday, October 2, 2005
Journal

10:15 p.m.

Wow. Busy day. Right now I feel irritable. Several people have rubbed me the wrong way today. Intellectually, I understand that this is only to be expected when living with 700+ people in a single room and not having taken a day off yet (by my choice). Emotionally, it's still difficult.

I got up this morning and drove to HQ for the mental health staffing. They assigned me to the base again. I argued for being put in the field—I was eager to get back to East Biloxi—but was unsuccessful. I was walking out the door to go back to the base when I was instead assigned to a *Hot Shot* call that came in. *Hot Shot* is the ARC version of a mental health mobile crisis unit—where a mental health professional goes into the community with the intention of de-escalating a crisis.

The Hot Shot I was assigned to involved a family who was having trouble with their adolescent and needed mental health assistance. ARC systems being what they were, it took me 1.5 hours to get out on the road. It took me about an hour-plus to find the location, as most of the street signs were still down. Since I wasn't getting anywhere fast, I took the opportunity to stop at re-supply stations (*bulk distribution* in ARC lingo) and stores—both to get directions as well as to find out what people needed.

After more driving, I found the address, which turned out to be in a trailer park set up by FEMA. FEMA had moved people from Pass Christian whose homes had been destroyed, and put them in this mobile home park except that FEMA apparently forgot to factor in people's needs like medication and food. I was the first Red Cross person that these people had seen since immediately after the storm—quite a scary thought! Many people living in the park had not had medication since the storm (over five weeks ago now!). I met with as many families as I could, gathered as much information as I could and called it back in to HQ.

I spent the rest of the day stopping at houses around Kiln and distributing what I had (mostly juices, sports drinks and some food). It was very hot today, so I tried to drink a lot of liquids myself. I met a large number of wonderful people, all of whom were very grateful and seemed pleased to hear that the rest of us hadn't forgotten them. It was easy for me to forget that these folks had no access to any media sources—no cable, no Internet, few radios. Consequently, they had no idea how the world was responding to their plight. I tried to fill them in as best as I could.

After a long day, I got back to HQ and was debriefed by people from several different departments who promised to get food, medicine and supplies out to the trailer park as soon as possible. As frustrating as it had been to see how those people had been dumped in trailer parks by FEMA with little to no coordination with the Red Cross, I felt like I had done something worthwhile: I had used my community-based skills to find people in distress and get them the help that they needed.

As I write this, I'm struck by remembering how worried I had been about being safe, and how the ARC trainers in Montgomery had stressed that we would never—*never*—be deployed alone. Yet here I was, driving out through the back roads of southern Mississippi by myself. Strangely, I felt safe. I also felt like I could move faster (sometimes getting groups of volunteers to move together took an exceptional amount of time) and serve people quicker on my own.

Sunday, October 2, 2005
Blog (by Patrick)

Sunday

Tim called just now. He spent the day working in Kiln, Mississippi. He was working with families who have moved up there from Bay St. Louis—which sounds as if it was wiped out! The government is setting up trailer homes for about 400 families. Tim is doing all right, drinking lots of water because of the heat, and trying to help all he can. Tim said that Kiln had hit the trifecta in disasters—first Katrina, then Rita, and then tornados! Tim said he was O.K., but you can hear in his voice that he has a lot to process about what is down there.

Katrina
At a Glance

Over 5 million people lost electricity due to Katrina, which is like shutting off power to the entire city of Boston.

Monday, October 3, 2005
Journal

A Typical Day at the Base

I've been told that I'll be assigned to the base for the next several days. Remembering the quick switch that happened to me with being assigned to East Biloxi, I'm taking this news with a grain of salt. At first I was bothered by this posting, thinking that I would be more effective out in the field, but I quickly realized that there is an enormous amount that a Mental Health volunteer can do around the base shelter.

The morning begins at 6:00 a.m. when they throw the switch that turns on the enormous industrial light fixtures hanging throughout this warehouse serving as our bedroom. I find these lights to be so jarring that I generally prefer to set my alarm so I'm up and moving before the lights flash on. Once the lights are on, the base camp quickly comes to life, with people getting up, getting dressed and getting ready for another day in the southern Mississippi heat.

Old & New

Many people are on their cell phones as soon as they get up, coordinating their plans for the day with other volunteers. I find myself wondering what ARC deployment was like before the advent of cell phones. In fact, this entire Katrina operation seems to be a blending of the old and the new, both in terms of people and technology. There is definitely an "old guard" contingency of ARC volunteers, people who have been with the ARC for decades. Most of them strongly believe that they know "the way things must be done" and—by God—no record-breaking national disaster is going to change that.

A veteran ARC volunteer told me that some of the old guard use the ARC as a sort of vacation. Going off to serve punch and cookies to victims of small scale disasters seems to be a way of escaping the harsh northern winters for some senior citizens. There's certainly nothing wrong with that in itself, but it appears that Katrina is not offering the old guard the typical sort of amenities—and some of the old guard are not pleased.

Thinking about the old guard, a ridiculous scene flashes to mind. Recalling comedian Bill Cosby's routine about how his grandfather used to brag about having to walk to school uphill (both ways!), I imagine myself volunteering with the ARC thirty years from now, telling a brand new volunteer a similar story: "You think you have it bad here? My first ARC deployment was Katrina, yessir, and we had it tough there, I'll tell you. You wouldn't be complaining about [*whatever*] if you'd been in Katrina!"

I've also noticed that some of the ARC volunteers—even some of the managers and supervisors—have trouble thinking in more global, systemic terms. They do what they are told and that's that, preferring instead to "do it as we've always done," as one veteran told me a few days ago. While there is certainly value in attending to tradition, the fact has quickly become apparent to many new ARC volunteers (myself included) that some ARC standard operating procedures need to evolve quickly in the face of a national disaster of Katrina's scale.

Back to the Schedule ...

The process of providing effective mental health support is first and foremost all about relationships, so I spend a fair amount of time each day cultivating these relationships. I do this by going around meeting and talking to the various people who are spending their volunteer time (or paid time, for some) keeping the base up and running. It's a balancing act between strategy and intimacy. I've found it very important to use people's first names here, since I'm amazed at how many people neglect to do this.

People working on the base include the cook staff, the laundry personnel, and the Smoke Jumpers who manage traffic control and perform additional duties around the base. There's also a team of strapping young men who help distribute the enormous bag lunches to all the volunteers every day and also pass out the bags and bags and bags of ice that are needed to keep liquids and food cold and fresh in this sweltering Mississippi heat. Finally, the shelter staff is a dedicated group of volunteers working around the clock to make this space as comfortable as possible for the other volunteers.

I often take a good chunk of the morning to go around and touch base with all of these folks—very informally—chatting about the weather, ARC grapevine gossip and the like, and I feel that the time is well invested. On several occasions, at least one member from all of the groups I mentioned above has come to me with a mental health concern, either about themselves or someone on their team. I've been finding myself working especially close with the Smoke Jumpers, who, as gate keepers for the disaster relief volunteer part of the base, have been especially busy. The shelter staff is another group of people with whom I've been spending a lot of time, talking about problems or concerns that inevitably arise when trying to keep 700+ people happy and comfortable. All in all, my experience has been that practically every volunteer laboring to keep the base running is professional, hard-working and pleasant to work alongside.

Most days, I also spend part of the morning touching base

with those who stay behind in their cots. Sometimes these are people who are simply taking a day off and sleeping in. Other times, the person on the cot may be someone who is feeling very overwhelmed simply stayed in bed. These folks I spent more time with, supporting them as best I can, as well as making sure their supervisors know where they are and what their status is. Sometimes the folks in bed are actually physically sick. I try to bring these folks drinks throughout the day and check in on them from time to time. Several volunteers have become so ill that, in consultation with the medical team, we've made arrangements to have them transported to the hospital.

Afternoons

During the afternoons, things quiet down on base. This is the lull period of the day, leaving me time to work on any projects I might create—or even to catch up on my sleep with a nap. One afternoon I spent simply gathering information about the base. The Seabee Command has been kind enough to extend full base privileges to the ARC volunteers, and I had heard rumors that there was a gym, golf course, PX station, church/chapel and more on base. Up to this point in time, there hasn't been any centralized information that I could find in the staff shelter. Everything seemed to rely on word-of-mouth, with valuable information that could be of enormous use to new volunteers being lost every time the "veterans" completed their tours of duty.

I wanted to create a resource guide similar to what you find when you check into a hotel room—something with all the information written down for all the volunteers to use. I was able to find a good map of the base and went around and found all the available facilities. The most difficult of those for me personally were the churches. I've heard that the Roman Catholic mass was celebrated every day on base. I was looking forward to attending mass, but when I stopped in the chapel, I was overwhelmed with the feeling that if I went to mass, I would begin to cry uncontrollably. I still have too many days to get through for me to have the luxury of breaking down, so I decide to skip mass. Wanting to avoid mass is quite a strange experience to me, as attending mass is something that I usually find very comforting. Perhaps "coming home" to the familiarity of mass for me is too stark a contrast to the strangeness of the devastation and destruction in which I live every day down here.

Evenings

Evening is when the base comes alive. Volunteers begin coming home for dinner around 4:30 p.m. and this is when the mental health teams gets very busy. For my part, I try as unobtrusively as I can to circulate among the returning volunteers—talking, laughing and listening. As in all things human, the grapevine continues to be a powerful tool. I touch base with as many returning volunteers as I can each evening, listening for gossip about who might have had a particularly stressful day. The ARC grapevine works so well that I often hear about significant events happening in the field well before the volunteers who are involved return to the base. For example, one problem that occurred with some regularity in the ARC shelters in the community was the problem of psychiatric patients—people with serious mental health issues. These patients would find their way into the shelters set up throughout the community and often begin to decompensate as they did not have access to their medicine. The ARC staff would work hard to get these people to the hospital. The hospital (being undersupplied and understaffed) would often turn around and discharge these patients back to the same ARC shelter, effectively setting up a vicious cycle. One day this week, the ARC grapevine was abuzz about a community shelter that had a particularly unpleasant episode with a psychiatric patient. By the time the mental health team member who was working that particular community shelter returned to the base, she was surprised to discover that I already knew most of the details.

With so many people living in such close proximity, the ARC has to stay on top of any infectious diseases spreading. There are bottles of hand sanitizer positioned all around the encampment, and most people use them quite liberally. (Note added after returning home: To this day, the scent of certain types of hand sanitizer quickly brings me back to my ARC days in the Deep South.)

During the evenings, volunteers eat dinner and then relax in various ways—mostly talking either to other ARC volunteers or to folks back home on their cell phones. I focus on walking around and chatting with people. After a few days of doing this, I noticed that there seems to be sort of a sixth sense kicking in, telling me which volunteers might be in need of a little more support than others. It's difficult to put my finger on it, but there's something in the way a few people sit and stand and move that tells me they're experiencing higher levels of stress. Whenever I see someone like this, I try to gently approach them to see how they're doing ... and more often than not, the person seems to be very glad to have someone to talk with about their day. For example, one day I noticed a woman sitting on her cot with her arms wrapped tightly around her staring off into space. I approached her and began talking. Her name was Rita and she had been assigned to Waveland, Mississippi, one of the many towns that had been completely wiped off the face of the map by the storms.

"I've been working in Waveland for several days," said Rita "and thought I was handling things pretty well. This morning I was walking down the street ..."

I sat silently as she began to cry.

Smiling through her tears, Rita continued. "It seems so silly. I was walking down the street when I came across a baby doll. It was very similar to the kind of doll I had growing up ... and well, I just lost it."

Night

I generally "work the floor" until lights-out at ten, and then I often move whatever conversation I'm having in the sleeping areas to the dining tents outside, which stay lit all night. I often use this time to informally debrief shelter staff members, talking about events that have gone on during the day. Then I try to fit in a short period of journaling and meditation, and then I'm off to bed myself. I'm effectively on-call throughout the night for the shelter staff, so I get what sleep I can.

Katrina
At a Glance

Many people who lived through the aftermath of Katrina will experience Posttraumatic Stress Disorder (PTSD), a mental condition that often follows exposure to extreme traumatic stressors.

Tuesday, October 4, 2005
Journal

An Unexpected Development

Nighttime is prime time for mental health services on the base, because evening is when the base comes alive. People return from long days in the field and are hungry, tired and ready to blow off some steam. Fortunately, the food on base is simply marvelous, and people seem to change dramatically for the better after eating a wonderful meal. Nowhere could I have hoped to find a better a better example of good food feeding the soul as well as the body.

My understanding is that the main role of mental health volunteers is to support the ARC volunteers, and as I work the base, I can see why. The volunteers often come back to base displaying signs of Post Traumatic Stress Syndrome (PTSD). Those who are willing to talk about it—mostly the women— describe symptoms ranging from loss of sleep, to loss of appetite, to nightmares, to full-blown flashbacks (which is where you are remembering an event so vividly, you are almost there again).

In addition to the PTSD symptoms that the volunteers are reporting, another theme has begun to emerge—one that I hardly expected. Besides responding to the shocking devastation, many of the ARC volunteers are appalled at the levels of poverty they are seeing firsthand.

When you drive through the devastation in southern Mississippi, it is not uncommon to see the entire front of a house ripped off. Driving past these houses, one can easily see inside—very much like a life-sized dollhouse. As you might expect, some of the insides of these houses are in shambles, but others are surprisingly untouched. The problem is that many of the good people of Mississippi are stunningly poor. Having worked as a case manager and home-based therapist, I have seen the highly impoverished conditions that people live in back home in Northeast Ohio. For me, Mississippi is not that much different. However, many of the ARC volunteers come from the more affluent part of American society. A large majority of the volunteers I've spoken with here have never seen the living conditions of the lower socio-economic levels of America. In a country where one out of six children live in poverty, some ARC volunteers apparently believe poverty to be something that happens in far-off lands—not in the United States of America!

I've had a number of conversations with ARC volunteers who are as disturbed by the poverty they're seeing as they are by the storm's destruction. "I can't believe Americans live like this," is a refrain I've heard many times over the past several days. On one hand I'm saddened by seeing the volunteers so disturbed, but on the other hand, I'm glad they're being exposed to the underbelly of America that they did not even know existed.

Wednesday, October 5, 2005
Journal

Mars, Arms, Rams, Wars

There was a problem at the shelter today and one of the ARC shelter staff members was walked off the base under armed guard. In fact, several volunteers have been escorted off the base under such conditions in the past few days.

While I cannot go into detail about the offense that the staff member committed, rest assured that it was nowhere near the level of behavior that most people would consider the need for an armed escort. After watching the escort accompany this gentle woman off the base, I went to the head of the staff shelter and expressed my concerns about the armed detail. I don't think that watching ARC colleagues being marched off by burly men brandishing automatic weapons will do wonders for the remaining volunteers' morale.

I spent a good part of the day talking to several people on the base about the possibility of changing the armed escort if someone needed to be taken off the base. I proposed the alternative of speaking one-to-one with the offending person (with the armed force waiting out of sight, in case they were needed) and seeing if the person would voluntarily leave the ARC base. I even offered to be the person who went in and talked to the volunteers who were having serious enough problems to be asked to leave the base.

My requests have been turned down at every step. I was given a number of different reasons, including that things needed to happen "a certain way," due to the fact that we're on a military base. While I fully appreciate and respect the hospitality that the Seabees are extending us, and I strongly support the need for a no-tolerance policy (such as when volunteers attempted to smuggle alcohol onto the base), I believe that invoking armed escorts for infractions of the rules is a recipe for disaster. Too much face is lost when you ask someone to leave base under an armed guard in front of their peers.

Note made after returning home: Sadly, this situation was never altered during my tour, leaving a bad taste in my mouth every time another incident occurred—and the process apparently continued after I left.

Thursday, October 6, 2005
Journal

Hardship Conditions

I'm beginning to understand why the ARC stressed "hardship conditions" so many times during orientation: apparently, some people have difficulty hearing information. As the mental health worker on the base, I've come into contact with several people who were thinking that this trip would be— well, I'm not sure what they were thinking when they signed up to come here.

For example, today the shelter staff came to me with a concern. A volunteer who arrived last night has been causing quite a commotion, and the staff asked if I could talk with her. They pointed Sally out to me, who was sitting on her cot, quietly rocking herself.[1] I went up to Sally and introduced myself.

"I can't believe it!" Sally said in a near shriek. "I simply can't live in these conditions!"

I asked her what was wrong, and she launched into her story—a long story, somewhat rambling and not always coherent. Remembering how overwhelmed I had felt upon first arriving

---

1. Not her real name. Names and other information have been changed through this chapter to protect confidentiality.

at the base, I gave Sally the benefit of the doubt. Slowly and gently I tried to steer her monologue in some direction that had anything to do with Gulfport, Mississippi. But she was not to be deterred, and I found myself thinking, "The ARC screeners sure missed this one." Based on the number of volunteers who were deployed so rapidly, I would certainly give the ARC screeners the benefit of the doubt, understanding that they couldn't catch everyone who might not be fit for ARC duty.

As Sally talked, I remembered a conversation I'd had with the director of the Lake County (Ohio) Red Cross Chapter before I left. He did a great job of calming my nerves that day by answering my many questions and giving me a brief history of mental health's involvement with the ARC. Thinking back, I remembered his parting words, which he spoke with a smile: "Expect everything."

Meanwhile, Sally was still talking. I gently asked her what was wrong, right here, right now, in this moment.

"The problem is," she said, leaning forward conspiratorially, "there are *men* here. And there are no *beds*." Being a card-carrying member of the offending gender (which Sally seemed to graciously overlook), I took a deep breath and asked her what she'd thought before she left things were going to be like.

"I thought that I would at least have my own room," she said. "They never told me about this," she added, waving her hand in the air to indicate our extremely co-ed sleeping arrangements. When I found out that Sally had been deployed through Montgomery, I smiled to myself, remembering how many times "hardship conditions" had been mentioned at the Montgomery ARC HQ when I was there.

After talking with her for a few more minutes, it became very obvious that Sally was clearly out of her element. We talked through her options and she decided that she wanted to go home, a decision that I whole-heartedly supported. I thanked her for her time and then spoke to the shelter staff director. Together we made arrangements to get Sally out-processed and sent home.

Screening people for early discharge has turned out to be a task that keeps me quite busy. I was never given any specific criteria for discharging people, so I—and the other mental health workers serving with me—have pretty much created the process as we've been going along, using our best clinical judgment. While there has occasionally been some disagreement among the ARC mental health staff about when to allow a discharge, for the most part, most of us have been on the same page. Whenever I'm called upon to consider someone for an early discharge, my basic perspective is that a discharge is not mine to "allow." I don't think it is ethical to wield power in that way over people in the present situation. I much prefer to arrive at a mutually agreed upon decision between myself and the volunteer in question—except for Bobby.

Tanned, well-muscled and handsome, with a deep Southern drawl, Bobby and I met several days ago when he inserted himself into a conversation I was having with someone else. He's one of those people who seems friendly and affable at first, but the more I talked with him, the clearer it became that Bobby needed to be the center of conversation at all times. Telling people that he was a nurse, Bobby freely boasted and bragged about all the ARC disaster responses he'd been deployed on. He even claimed to have gone over to Thailand with the International Red Cross to help out with the tsunami earlier this year. Every time Bobby told one of his stories, I always felt a hollow "thud" in the pit of my stomach, so I had difficulty placing much stock in what he was saying.

Over the next few days, I heard several members of the shelter staff talking about Bobby—and usually not in very complimentary terms. In addition, Bobby had an unsettling habit of stepping into the mental health team's conversations. One of my team members had a particularly strong reaction to Bobby, often getting sucked into verbal sparring matches with him.

This morning one of the members of the Red Cross H.R. department came to me and asked me about assessing someone for possible discharge. Elly, a young lady of about twenty-five inquired how long I would need to assess an individual and asked about other details of the assessment process. As we talked, she began telling me some of H.R.'s concerns about a particular volunteer. A number of things she said began to sound familiar. As she ended with, "… and we're not even sure that this guy has the credentials that he says he does," I decided to hazard a guess.

"By any chance, is this guy's name Bobby?" I asked her.

Elly just stared at me. "That's exactly who I'm talking about."

I let her know that I was very familiar with him and that I was equally concerned about him. As we walked together, I unobtrusively pointed him out to her, just to confirm that we were talking about the same person, which we were. Then I told Elly that I wouldn't need to assess this particular fellow and that I would highly recommend immediate discharge for him. She thanked me for my time—and this evening I heard that Bobby has already been sent on his way home.

Amazingly, I have met very few people like Bobby or Sally (a tribute to the ARC screening process, I think.) The majority of people who've decided to go home ahead of schedule have had very legitimate reasons, spanning the entire range of human misfortune. Volunteers have sought early discharge for events like a death in the family, a very sick child, or a basement that inexplicably started leaking. Overall, my experience has been that the ARC volunteers take their jobs very seriously, and many of the people who have needed to leave early often said they feel very guilty about doing so.

When I'm working with someone who is transitioning home early, I view my role as being there to support them in their leaving and (hopefully) to help them experience as little shame as possible about going home early. I've certainly had a few tearful goodbyes with people as they left for the airport, and my heart has gone out to them. I hope they don't feel badly for very long. At least they made the effort to come down here to help. Hopefully they won't look back with any regrets.

Thursday, October 6, 2005
Blog (by Patrick)

Tim is Coming Home!

For the last several days, Tim has been on the Seabee's base, helping where he can. He has helped talk to other workers who might be having trouble coping with what is going on in the south. Tim is working long hours—usually 6:30 a.m. to 1:00 a.m. He is clear that he is doing these hours by choice, and he is pacing himself—taking naps and breaks so he does not burn out. I, for one, cannot wait to hear the stories of what Tim witnessed there. He flies out on Friday.

Katrina
At a Glance

In 2005, for the first time in its 44-year history, the U.S. Peace Corps worked *within* the borders of the U.S., primarily in states impacted by Katrina along the Gulf coast.

Friday, October 7, 2005
Journal

8:45 a.m.

Yahoo! I am going home to see my family! I can't believe that I haven't written in my journal since Sunday—but then again, maybe I can. The week has gone by unbelievably fast. I've spent most of this week assigned to the Seabee base, although I was in the field for parts of some days.

One morning, I spent a frustrating four-hour process of loading up a supply van and driving it to a supply point to support Mental Health colleagues—a process that would ordinarily take one hour at the most. Traffic is so horrific in Gulfport that any time you hit the road to drive anywhere, it can take an enormously long time. On another day, I spent an afternoon working at the Family Service Center (FSC) in the Singing River Mall in Gautier, Mississippi, again supporting the distribution of relief checks to residents. My experience at this FSC couldn't have been more different from my experience at the other FSC I described earlier. The FSC at the Singing River Mall had an amazing staff, led by a local ARC volunteer named Charlie (and Charlie—if you read this, I'd like to take you up on that fishing trip we talked about. Call me.). Between the police (a group of very sharp guys from Birmingham, Alabama), the ARC and the National Guard, they were running a highly professional FSC. Rather than remaining aloof, the police and National Guard were mingling with the residents, passing out drinks and chatting.

At this FSC I met an amazing group of Mississippians, most of whom rode out Hurricane Katrina in their houses. I spoke to a jazz guitarist (I'm a big fan of jazz guitar) who lost several prize instruments in the flood. I spoke to a woman who rode out the hurricane with 10 other people in a 22-foot boat tied to her house. Most moving for me was my conversation with a WWII veteran who broke into tears when I told him I was from Ohio—he was so profoundly touched by the response of the American people.

I spent yesterday at the base, orienting and introducing two women who were replacing me as mental health staff at the base—Deb who is from Findley, Ohio (at last, another Ohioan!) and Susan who is from California. Both Deb and Susan have a lot of enthusiasm and great ideas for what has become the largest staff shelter in the history of the ARC. I must admit that I was initially put out at being assigned to the base, seeing it as the equivalent of being benched during the World Series. However, over the past week I have really come to value the important work that needs to be done here on base. In fact, the mental health services for volunteers on the base has really become my baby. I like to think that my efforts on base had some impact on HQ's decision to now assign two mental health workers to the base. I know that I'm leaving my baby in excellent hands.

I finally got my hands on a massage table this week. I'm a certified massage professional and energetic body worker, practicing a form called Nervous System Energy Work (NSEW). I've spent several evenings giving ARC people massages and energy sessions. People seemed very grateful—they would start out very tense and I could feel them relax as our work progressed together. When I was doing energetic work, I noticed that people's kidney's seemed especially 'needy'—for lack of a better word—their kidneys seemed empty energetically.

A number of people that I worked on went to sleep very quickly. It was pretty weird—sometimes I get skeptical about all this energy stuff, but it seemed very profound in working with the ARC volunteers. At one point in time, I was working on six men who were sitting around a regular table—and each and every one of them went to sleep! How wild! Sadly, there were far more people who wanted bodywork than I could accommodate. We could have used a large number of massage/bodywork professionals to support the ARC staff at the end of each day.

I'm currently sitting at the Gulfport Airport, which is just coming back to life after having been closed because of the storms. I'm waiting for my flight home, and they just turned on the overhead music. The music sounds strange to me, because I haven't heard background music for several weeks now.

I find myself being concerned about my re-entry to everyday life. From where I'm sitting now, I'm imagining that everyday life will be somewhat strange. I think I need to keep it simple—go fishing and chop firewood.

I'm going to go read for a bit.

Katrina
At a Glance

In the aftermath of Katrina,
over 60,000 people volunteered
for the first time with the American
Red Cross—a number that would
fill Heinz Stadium in Pittsburgh,
Pennsylvania, home of the
Pittsburgh Steelers,
the 2005 Superbowl Champions.

Friday, October 7, 2005
Journal

2:30 C.S.T.

I am sitting in the Memphis airport waiting for my flight to Cleveland and home. There is a BBQ restaurant down the concourse that smells wonderful. I'm hungry, but I'm too tired to stand in the long line that has formed in front of the restaurant. That's one thing about the Red Cross—everything happens in a line. Some of the military folks who I spoke to said that the military is the same way.

As I watch people in the airport, people seem to be moving very fast, or at least with a different kind of fast than the Red Cross folks.

They're calling my flight. I'm going home.

Katrina
At a Glance

By April, 2006, the American Red Cross announced that they had received enough financial donations and pledges to cover the $2.116 billion costs for the ARC response to Hurricanes Katrina, Rita and Wilma.

Home Again,
Home Again.

Sunday, October 9, 2005
Journal

Home on Sunday

Hi all! I've been home for two days now, and still adjusting. I imagine "adjusting" will take some time. I find that I am very, *very* tired, and that doing even small things exhausts me quickly. I'm also experiencing a lot of the typical stress-related symptoms—finding it difficult to concentrate, not wanting to be around crowds of people, etc. As a clinical counselor, I know what the symptoms are, but experiencing them firsthand is very strange.

It has been wonderful to see my kids and my wife—I've missed them greatly. I got on the Aikido mat yesterday for a short practice, and that felt good too.

All in all, I'm just winding down a bit. I'm hoping to spend some time this week editing my journal and then I can post it— and pictures—on the web for all to see.

Katrina
At a Glance

Over 1,000 volunteer amateur ("ham") radio operators traveled to provide communication in areas where the normal communication infrastructure had been damaged or destroyed by the storm.

Monday, October 10, 2005
Blog

Seabee Camp

Hi all. I'm still putting things into perspective here at home. I was looking up some Katrina information on the web, and came across an article that describes the food I got to eat at the Seabee base.

The article mentions a fellow by the name of Gary Stewart from Idaho, who I had the pleasure and privilege of meeting. Gary's job was to greet volunteers coming onto the base and to direct them appropriately. For most of us, this would be considered a dead-end position, but not for Gary. Gary welcomed us back to the base each and every night with a friendly smile and a rousing recitation of the evening's menu. I can't begin to tell you how much I looked forward to seeing Gary's face each night. If anyone out there knows Gary, thank him profusely and buy him a beer for me, please.

If you read the article, it mentions having a margarita night. I was there for the margarita night (non-alcoholic, of course), and it was wonderful—just what people seemed to need.

Katrina
At a Glance

In the 2005 hurricane season,
the American Red Cross distributed
34 million meals, which would feed
everyone in the state of California,
the most densely populated
state in the U.S.

Monday, October 17, 2005
Blog

Still Getting Back Into Things...

Hi all! Well, I've been home for over one week now, and I'm still trying to get my feet on the ground. It's been pretty weird. Even though I've was only (!) there for two weeks, I find myself experiencing a number of symptoms of PTSD (Post-Traumatic Stress Disorder). Minor stuff, but still somewhat troublesome. I still continue to be very tired. Sometimes the slightest sound or smell will take me back to Mississippi. Lots of other stuff, too. I've managed to get a massage and see my therapist, and both of those sessions have helped tremendously. My family and I also went on a nature hike on Sunday at Penitentiary Glen—part of the Lake County Metroparks. It was very beautiful in the woods, and the colors of the Ohio woods in autumn continue to soothe me.

I just began writing out my experiences from the journal that I kept. I met with a great deal of resistance in writing it out, and, procrastinator that I am, put it off for several days. I am finally getting down to work, and the journal is already bringing back memories that I had already forgotten.

Katrina
At a Glance

As of March, 2006,
about 16,000 federal personnel
had been deployed to help
areas along the Gulf coast.

By March, 2006,
about 115,000 U.S. troops
had been deployed to
fight in Iraq.

Sunday, March 19, 2006
Blog

The Gestalt of Crisis Intervention

Hi all! It's been months since I've written, but I still continue to ... what's the word? ... *incorporate* my experience down South into the rest of my life. Today I received a request, from a list-serv that I belong to, for information about Gestalt psychology & crisis intervention by a professional who was responding to a crisis in the Philippines. Here's what I wrote:

§§§

I spent two weeks last fall down in Southern Mississippi with the American Red Cross working with people who lived through Hurricanes Katrina and Rita (most of whom disliked being referred to as "survivors," so I'm avoiding that term). While I'm continuing to debrief about my own experience there (even six months later), I'd like to share some insights that I found helpful during my time as a Disaster Worker.

1. GESTALT IS PERFECT FOR CRISIS WORK.

I found Gestalt to be a *very* powerful tool to apply when I was working in Mississippi. For me, the strongest part of this powerful tool was focusing on the relationship in the present moment (physical process was a close second—keep breathing!). Both critical incident stress debriefing and counseling interventions were required–with different interventions for different people.

There were other mental health workers there who took a decidedly non-Gestalt, gung-ho, "See-this-clipboard-I'm-carrying-I'm-a-mental-health-worker-and-I-can-fix-all-your-problems" type of approach, which seemed to serve only to alienate just about everyone in the room, present company included. It also taught me why we mental health professionals often get a bad reputation—because we sometimes deserve it.

In my opinion, deciding which interventions to "extend" to people before you even meet them is not very helpful. The power of Gestalt, for me, lies in its emphasis on being present in the moment and being willing to engage in authentic dialog with people. Being fully present in authentic dialog is far scarier for most professionals, I'll guess. It would be so much easier to "know" what to do—and much less effective.

2. TO SUPPORT OTHERS, SUPPORT YOURSELF.

When I was working in Mississippi, I quickly discovered that, at some levels, the work was much simpler than I expected, while at other levels it was completely exhausting.

The work was simpler in the sense that, as an experienced clinician used to working at deeper levels with long-term clients, I experienced many of the interventions I used in Mississippi as somewhat "light," and I was worried that they were too superficial.

When I sought feedback from the people with whom I worked, they were strongly supportive of the Gestalt approach I was using, saying things like, "I felt like you were with me the whole time," and, "You weren't trying to 'fix' me like some other people tried to do."

At the same time, while the crisis work in Mississippi felt "lighter" compared to the work I usually do, I found myself quickly getting exhausted after only a few hours of doing such work— and I'm used to working very long days. The lesson: clinically, crisis work is technically simple work—and emotionally quite exhausting.

3. MEET PEOPLE WHERE THEY ARE—HERE & NOW.

Another suggestion that I would strongly make is taking a page from community-based care—go and meet the people where they are (a very Gestalt perspective, I think). While engaging in community-based care, the American Red Cross wisely suggested that we *not* identify ourselves as mental health workers to the general population, since doing so only seems to get people moving away from us as fast as they can. Here in the U.S., mental health treatment has a rather negative stigma. I do not know how mental health services are perceived in the Philippines—you're more of the expert on that. Adjust accordingly.

If you're working at an evacuation shelter, I think the least helpful thing to do is to set up a table/area as "mental health" and sit behind the table waiting for people to come to you (if that is the only thing you do). When I was working shelters, I found it much more effective to simply wander around talking to people. One doesn't need to hang out in a crisis shelter too long before you quickly begin to identify stress responses in people. Wandering up to someone who looks stressed and starting a conversation often seemed to work wonders—far better than waiting for them to come over to the mental health table.

4. WORK IN COMMUNITY.

I would, of course, identify myself as a mental health worker to the other workers in the shelter. Other staff members could then act as additional sets of eyes and ears. When staff members saw people getting stressed, they could notify me or another mental health worker so that we could quietly intervene before things escalated.

Something else I discovered was the importance of my role as "on-the-job-trainer" for the non-mental health staff. Under stress, *everything* began looking like a crisis to some shelter staff. I often helped the shelter staff sort through what kind of situations needed to be addressed immediately and which ones did not. For example, I found that *anyone* crying *at all* was often cause for quite an alarm among the shelter staff. Helping to debrief the shelter staff in the moment, by educating them that (it almost seems silly to write this) it is normal for people to cry in stressful situations, went a long way toward avoiding an escalation during several situations.

5. DISCOVER THE ZEN OF CRISIS WORK.

In Mississippi, I learned that every interaction is important—a very Zen idea, that. In addition to the more straight-forward mental health interventions, I also had conversations with people around cooking, fishing, travel and even cars (which I know next-to-nothing about). These conversations typically felt fairly innocuous to me. I cannot begin to tell you how many times people would come up to me later and say something like:

"Thank you SO much for talking about [insert topic here]! I felt SO much better after having a NORMAL conversation."

These interactions taught me not to underestimate the powerful healing that occurs when people can have "normal" conversations in the midst of a crisis. Every true conversation (read: *genuine contact* in Gestalt language) is important in a crisis.

I hope something in my words helps support you in your work. Please feel free to contact me if I can be of further help. You'll be in my prayers.

Best of luck,

Tim

§§§

Sunday, March 26, 2006
Blog

Funny...

It is funny how sunlight can play with the bare branches of an early spring Ohio day and look amazingly like a late fall afternoon in Mississippi. The lighting, the color of the branches—all the same. Amazing! I was just looking out the window at some of the trees and shrubs that surround my house, and found myself remembering ...

§§§

One day, I was driving down a Mississippi backroad somewhere near Kiln, and I stopped to ask for directions. In front of the house, a large group of men were cutting down some trees that had been torn out by the post-Rita tornados that had hit the area. In the back of the house, another group of men were cutting apart an enormous tree that had fallen right on top of a barn. I passed around sports drink for everyone, and we sat and talked a bit.

As I was leaving, one of the men (who's gorgeous Cajun/ French name I can't recall) pointed to a large damaged white farmhouse across the road, and said, "I really appreciate what all y'all in the Red Cross have done for us here in ol' Miss. If'n ever you need any help, y'all just knock on that farmhouse door—even if it's 2:00 in the morning—and I'll do anything I can to help y'all."

§§§

I hope that if that my community is ever damaged in a natural disaster, I'll have the wisdom and grace to extend an invitation to the disaster workers to knock on my door—even at 2:00 a.m. in the morning.

Tuesday, June 13, 2006
Blog

Hurricane Season (Again...)

Today the media is playing up the fact that it is hurricane season again. Folks I've talked to who have been in southern Mississippi recently say there's still much to be rebuilt. I find myself getting frustrated with the media as it continues to focus almost exclusively on New Orleans, when the reality of the situation is that many more cities, towns and villages were impacted by the 2005 hurricanes—far beyond New Orleans.

A friend of mine is vacationing in Florida this week and a tropical storm is predicted to hit land. I've been surprised at the force of my concern for him, especially as the storm threatened to turn into a hurricane.

Strange.

Katrina
At a Glance

Hurricane Katrina was the costliest and most destructive natural disaster in U.S. history.

Pictures

A Note about the Pictures

Deciding to include these pictures was a difficult decision for me. The reviewers who looked at this book prior to publication were very divided about the inclusion of pictures—some wanted more, believing that a picture is truly worth a thousand words. Other reviews were opposed to including any pictures, believing that doing so might be insensitive to the residents of Mississippi.

Both groups are probably right.

The Red Cross explicitly trained volunteers to be very senstive about taking pictures—and rightly so. Imagine having your house destroyed in a natural disaster and having people jump out of their cars to take your picture for months and months.

All things considered, I have decided to include pictures in the service of providing people with a small glimpse of what happened in the southern U.S. states during the 2005 hurricane season. Following the Red Cross' lead, I have tried to be careful in my selection of pictures. If anyone finds these pictures insensitive, I beg that you recall Shakespeare's words spoken by the fairy spirit Puck in *A Midsummer Night's Dream*:

If we shadows have offended,
Think but this, and all is mended:
That you have but slumbered here,
While these visions did appear.

As Puck suggests, sometimes my time in Mississippi seems like a dream—or nightmare, more accurately.

But the hurricane season of 2005 did indeed happen ... and we must never forget.

Leaving my family

ARC HQ Montgomery—
inside an abandoned Kmart

Signs & pictures at ARC HQ

"Team Biloxi"— the author (Ohio),
Teresa (Alaska), & John (Illinois)

On the road to Biloxi—
first signs of damage

More damage

Gulfport, Mississippi

Biloxi/Gulfport ARC HQ—
A Shriner's Hall

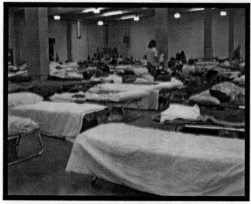

One Bedroom Warehouse—
sleeps 700

In East Biloxi.
This was someone's house.

A mess.
People were still living in the 2nd story apartment.

Driving through neighborhoods
marked with "X's" was creepy.

*East Biloxi. There was a indescribable smell in the air that
a military colleague said was decaying flesh.*

*Oceanfront property.
First two floors washed away by the sea.*

The foundation of a house.
Imagine seeing this over and over—for miles.

Some of the houses along the ocean in Biloxi were said
to have been built before the Civil War.

*The good people of Mississippi seemed to do a
marvelous job of keeping their sense of humor.*

*See the car in the right of the picture?
Those floating casinos the media kept talking about were enormous—
far larger than I thought they would be ...*

... but not so big that a hotel couldn't stop one!

*With water surges up to 30 feet, most of the tree branches
were draped with debris, giving some areas the feeling
of a demented Halloween party.*

Sometime it was hard to tell where I was.
This is near Waveland, I think.

Some places were hit by two hurricanes and several tornadoes.
One young lady I met told me excitedly about getting to see a cow fly t
hrough the air during one a tornado.

*Seeing trees on top of houses was a common sight
as I drove around Kiln, Mississippi.*

North of Pass Christian

Final
Musings

Some Final Musings

Words simply fail to describe the enormity of the destruction caused by the 2005 Hurricane season. Even when I personally saw the destruction along the southern coast of Mississippi, I could barely believe my own eyes. As a result of these storms, countless people were relocated around the country and property damage was suffered in the billions of dollars. The psychological, financial, emotional and physical scars will be with us for years to come. Everyone—volunteers, workers and residents alike—will remember these events for the rest of their lives.

While so much more remains to be said, here are a few random musings that I'd like to leave you with:

§§§

Please remember that the impact of the storms of 2005 was felt across the United States—far beyond New Orleans.

§§§

§§§

My experiences in Mississippi gave me a profound appreciation for combat veterans. After only two weeks in a hardship area, I experienced PTSD symptoms for months after my return—and nobody had been shooting at me. One can scarcely even imagine what it would be like to be in the military, to go to a foreign country, kill people and have them try to kill you, return home and be expected to act "normal."

§§§

This country owes a debt of gratitude to the gay/lesbian community, who frequently formed a strong backbone of many of the volunteer teams I met down south.

§§§

In my own process of healing from my volunteer time, I found that I needed to withdraw from contact with others outside a circle of family and close friends. Many of my ARC colleagues may not have heard from me in a very long time. To these colleagues I offer my sincere apologies and assure each and every one of you that you were never far from my heart in this past year.

§§§

After looking at the statistics surrounding the storms of 2005, I would like to humbly suggest that, as a nation, our priorities are—to use a clinical phrase—seriously out of whack. Regardless of whether you are a Republican, Democrat or Independent, simply look at the numbers (when you can find them) about how we as a nation choose to spend our—and our children's—money.

§§§

Acknowledgements

I am most grateful to Dr. Mary Ann Kraus, Psy. D., a profoundly wise therapist, for supporting me upon my return.

§§§

My deepest thanks to following people for emotional and other forms of support: my siblings Patrick and Mary; Deb Gurney, Kirste Carlson; all my friends and colleagues who held me in their thoughts and prayers; my new-found brother Gary Niki; and my ARC colleagues John Gallagher and Teresa Gochis.

§§§

Most of all, I am grateful and thankful to my wife and children for giving me up for two weeks in the fall of 2005 and allowing me to share my talents with others.

§§§

Websites

For the Katrina at a Glance Facts, I primarily used the following websites:

American Red Cross:
http://www.redcross.org

FEMA:
http://www.fema.gov

U.S. Department of Defense:
http://www.defenselink.mil

U.S. Department of Homeland Security:
http://www.dhs.gov/dhspublic/index.jsp

The article from the Idaho Statesman that featured Gary Stewart can be found at:
http://www.idahostatesman.com/apps/pbcs.dll/
article?AID=/20051004/NEWS01/510040360/1001/NEWS

Statistics are current as of summer, 2006.
I encourage you to check the facts for yourself.

Tim's on-going blog:
www.leadingpeople.blogspot.com

Tim's website:
www.timwarneka.com

ABOUT THE AUTHOR

Regarded as an expert in human performance, Tim Warneka is the founder of *The Black Belt Consulting Group* and the creator of the *Black Belt Way*, an innovative new approach to leadership that combines the strengths of Emotional Intelligence with the power of the revolutionary non-violent martial art of Aikido to create success with individuals, groups, teams & organizations.

Photo: Patrick Warneka

Tim is the author of the internationally acclaimed *Leading People the Black Belt Way: Conquering the Five Core Problems Facing Leaders Today*. Tim and his brother Patrick are currently at work on an updated urban interpretation of the *Tao Te Ching* for leaders.

A leadership coach, organizational consultant, clinical counselor, speaker & author, Mr. Warneka holds a bachelor's degree in psychology; a master's degree in counseling; a black belt in the revolutionary, non-violent martial art of Aikido; post-graduate training from the world-famous Gestalt Institute of Cleveland; and is an adjunct instructor at several colleges.

For more information, visit Tim on-line at:
www.timwarneka.com.

Also by Tim Warneka...

At last, a book that shows you the secrets of Black Belt Leaders! **LEADING PEOPLE THE BLACK BELT WAY** offers an exciting new approach to leadership that combines the strength of Emotional Intelligence with the power of the revolutionary non-violent martial art of Aikido. Packed with proven leadership strategies, here's your chance to acquire powerful, street-smart strategies to increase performance, experience greater life satisfaction and do more with less!

Leading People
the
Black Belt
Way

Conquering the Five Core Problems
Facing Leaders Today

Timothy H. Warneka

ISBN: 0-9768627-0-0 / $29.95 (HB)
ISBN: 0-9768627-1-9/ $19.95 (PB)

Praise for
Leading People the Black Belt Way...

"Being deeply aware of yourself and your surroundings, called mindfulness, is a major predictor of effective leadership and management at all levels. Tim Warneka's adaptation of martial arts philosophy and practice awakens the reader to fascinating and helpful techniques to increase your mindfulness."

—**RICHARD E. BOYATZIS**, Professor, Case Western Reserve University and ESADE, and co-author with Daniel Goleman and Annie McKee of the international best-seller, **Primal Leadership**, and more recently with Annie McKee, **Resonant Leadership.**

"...a valuable addition to the literature certain to impact many people's lives."

—**RICHARD STROZZI HECKLER**, Fifth degree Aikido black belt, world famous leadership coach and author, **Being Human at Work.**

"...a highly practical guide for leaders in all walks of life."

—**EDWIN C. NEVIS**, President, Gestalt International Study Center

Price subject to change. Available through your local bookstore, on-line retailers and from Asogomi Publishing International at www.asogomi.com.

Printed in the United States
900040LV000004B/374/A